Loose Cannons

Loose Cannons

Devastating Dish
from the World's Wildest Women

Autumn Stephens

MJF BOOKS
NEW YORK

Published by MJF Books
Fine Communications
Two Lincoln Square
60 West 66th Street
New York, NY 10023

Loose Cannons
Library of Congress Catalog Card Number 99-70061
ISBN 1-56731-319-1

This edition published by arrangement with Conari Press.
Cover Design: Ame Beanland
Book Design: Jennifer Brontsema

Manufactured in the United States of America on acid-free paper
MJF Books and the MJF colophon are trademarks of Fine Creative Media, Inc.

10   9   8   7   6   5   4   3   2   1

Contents

66 I got what I have now through knowing the right time to tell terrible people when to go to hell. **99**

—LESLIE CARON

The Oral Sex

Strong? You bet. Silent? Never. From notorious 15th-century widow Lucrezia Borgia ("My husbands have been very unlucky") to her 20th-century soulmate Lorena Bobbitt ("He doesn't wait for me to have an orgasm . . . so I pull[ed] back the sheets and then I did it"), no force of nature has ever prevented a fiercely opinionated femme from making her point.

Indeed, fear of a furious female tongue has been known to set a less-than-secure man to shaking in his Hush Puppies . . . which is NOT, needless to say, a situation your average dude is really apt to dig. Hence, we imagine, the old saw about "whistling girls and crowing hens." According to that dire dark-age ditty, you'll recall, chicks who made use of their vocal cords were practically predestined to "come to some bad end." (Or, as Sharon Stone so succinctly opined, "If you have a vagina and a point of view, that's a deadly combination.")

In our book, however, the stiff upper lip (not the flapping yap) is the truly lethal taboo. As four out of five ersatz MDs agree—or would, if they actually existed—it's a woman's omissions, not her emissions, that tend to be seriously toxic. Air your attitude, we say, and you'll wind up with a better job, smarter friends, and a lower level of stress. (Well, a lower level of stress, anyway.)

Few ailments, after all, are more fatal than a lingering case of lockjaw.

1.

$\mathcal{E}$ffusive
$\mathcal{E}$gotists

66 I myself am more divine than any I see. **99**

> —*Magnificent* MARGARET FULLER, *in an 1838 letter to Ralph Waldo Emerson. Brought up to hobnob with Harvard men, the immodest intellectual was known for her sky-high IQ . . . and equally expansive ego.*

66 I have often wished I had time to cultivate modesty.
But I am too busy thinking about myself. **99**

> —*Poet* EDITH SITWELL, *letter-perfect in the role of eccentric English Dame.*

" I think I am one of the few who gives our country any voice of its own. **"**

  —GEORGIA O'KEEFFE. *Sure, a single room might do for some. Not so, however, the self-touting symbolist who posthumously scored an entire edifice of her own: the first accredited US museum devoted to the ouevre of a woman artist.*

" No one working in the English language now comes close to my exuberance, my passion, my fidelity to words. **"**

  —*Novelist* JEANNETTE WINTERSON, *narcissist extraordinaire.*

66 I totally and completely admit, with no qualms at all, my ego-mania, my selfishness, coupled with a really magnificent voice. **99**

—*Soprano* LEONTYNE PRICE: *a prima donna, and proud of it.*

66 It is awesome to be an astrologer. **99**

—JOAN QUIGLEY, *astrologer.*

66 I've been in the twilight of my career longer than most people have had their career. 99

—MARTINA NAVRATILOVA, *a tennis pro for all seasons (not to mention all hours of the day).*

66 People are already pissed off at me because I'm athletic *and* beautiful, to be smart in addition . . . it's, like, too much. 99

—*Model* GABRIELLE REECE, *a woman of no modest gifts.*

" If I ever felt inclined to be timid . . . I would say to myself, 'You're the cleverest member of one of the cleverest families in the cleverest class of the cleverest nation in the world— why should you be frightened?' **"**

> —BEATRICE WEBB. *A big name in the English labor movement of the late 1800s, Webb worked for the good of the masses . . . but didn't entirely eschew elitism.*

66 I have the same goal I've had ever since I was a girl. I want to rule the world. **99**

66 I saw losing my virginity as a career move. **99**

66 Strong women leave big hickeys. **99**

   —*The mono-nomic* MADONNA, *determined from Day One to make her mark.*

66 I made myself Miss Manners. It was like Napoleon: You crown yourself because nobody else can do it. **99**

—JUDITH MARTIN, *America's self-made arbiter of socially correct conduct.*

66 Nobody, but nobody, is going to stop breathing on me. **99**

—VIRGINIA APGAR, MD. *A major name in pediatric medicine, all-powerful Apgar toted a spare set of tracheotomy tools in her pocketbook, along with a preserved fetus in a bottle (and possibly a lipstick or two).*

66 I am considered 'charmante' by the Frenchmen, 'lovely' by the Americans and 'really quite nice, you know,' by the English. 99

—*Surrogate first lady* PRISCILLA TYLER. *The self-assured stand-in for her ailing mother-in-law, twentyish Tyler was also considered quite the bee's knees by herself.*

66 When you know you're right, you don't care what others think. You know sooner or later it will come out in the wash. 99

—BARBARA MCCLINTOCK. *At the age of eighty-one, the boastful botanist finally reaped her well-deserved reward . . . in the form of a Nobel Prize.*

66 I know what's best for the President. I put him in the White House. He does well when he listens to me and poorly when he does not. 99

> —FLORENCE HARDING. *According to Mr. H, the nation's 29th head of state, his auto was the only thing the domineering "Duchess" didn't want to drive.*

66 What I am is a humanist before anything—before I'm a Jew, before I'm black, before I'm a woman. But somehow we are supposed to be *credits* to our race. The mere fact that I'm still around makes me a credit to my race, which is the human race. 99

—*Gladsome* WHOOPI GOLDBERG, *honored among homo sapiens.*

66 Bitches are aggressive, assertive, domineering, overbearing, strong-minded, spiteful, hostile, direct, blunt, candid, obnoxious, thick-skinned, hard-headed, vicious, dogmatic, competent, competitive, pushy, loud-mouthed, independent, stubborn, demanding, manipulative, egoistic, driven, achieving, overwhelming, threatening, scary, ambitious, tough, brassy, masculine, boisterous and turbulent. A Bitch takes shit from no one. You may not like her, but you cannot ignore her. 99

—JOREEN, *a big cheese in the Sisterhood movement of the Sixties, and you can go to heck right now if you think a Bitch needs to bother with a surname.*

66 A sense of power is the most intoxicating stimulant a mortal can enjoy. **99**

> —ELLEN SWALLOW RICHARDS. *The first American woman to obtain a science degree, Richards (MIT, class of 1873) mixed up her own potent concoctions in chemistry lab.*

66 I am too pretty to bother with an eyebrow pencil. **99**

> —CHAO LUAN-LUAN, *self-confident courtesan of 8th-century China.*

66 I'm not ugly. I'm cute as hell. 99

—CHRISTINE CRAFT. *The fortyish anchorwoman waged a landmark legal battle when she was bumped downstairs for not being, in either sense of the word, a babe.*

66 I see no cameras! *Where* are the cameras? 99

—*Such was the constant cry of* QUEEN MARY *of England, the consort who was* always *ready for her close-up.*

2.

*Beefin'
Beauties*

66 I never cared to be Miss America. I am so bored by it all. **99**

—MARGARET GORMAN CAHILL, *who received her tiresome tiara in 1921.*

66 Get enough sleep and enough sex. If you don't get enough of either, it will end up showing on your face. **99**

—*Newswoman* KIM HUME's *best beauty tip, with a nod (or a wink) in the direction of foxy Ben "Early to Bed, Early to Rise" Franklin.*

66 I'm not one of those little things. I have a butt and boobs. It's great. I sometimes tell people I weigh 10 pounds more than I actually do. 99

—*Couture freak* COURTNEY LOVE, *one grrrl who outgrew the Hole grunge gig.*

66 Everything you see, I owe to spaghetti. 99

—*La bella* SOPHIA LOREN, *a walking advertisement for carbo loading.*

66 I was raised on pork, and believe me, I'm healthy. **99**

—TINA TURNER, *R&B's best-preserved sexagenarian.*

66 Chubby Hubby ice cream—I can't say no anymore. **99**

—SIDNEY BIDDLE BARROWS, *the erstwhile Mayflower Madam, on the subject of her sole remaining vice.*

66 They say that inside every fat woman is a skinny woman waiting to get out. Well, all I can say is, I ate that bitch. 99

—THEA VIDALE, *carnivorous comedian.*

66 There are breast roles and there are nonbreast roles. For instance, when I was Stella in *A Streetcar Named Desire* on Broadway in 1988, I thought they were appropriate. 99

—*Full-figured (or not!)* FRANCES MCDORMAND, *an actress with more than one point of view.*

66 I'd never let my nipples show at a state function—I'd be frightened the old men would have heart attacks. 99

> —*Brazen* MARGARET TRUDEAU, *briefly the better (or worse) half of Canada's far more proper PM.*

66 I would rather dance completely nude than strut in half-clothed suggestiveness, as many women do today on the streets of America. 99

> —*An uncharacteristically demure* ISADORA DUNCAN. *Somehow, we doubt that iconoclastic Izzie would have flipped her wig had she lived to see (or model) the mini.*

66 Women in skirts should keep their knees together, not just for modesty but out of politeness, since few people really want a view of the undergarments of women sitting across from them. 99

—*Manners maven* PEGGY POST, *today's foremost theorist in the field of unintentional unmentionable sightings.*

66 Free your mind, and your bottom will follow. 99

—*The newly svelte* FERGIE *(aka Sarah Ferguson), yet another Royal who has trouble keeping track of her rear.*

66 Big buttocks are not a disease. **99**

—*Popular proverb among Luyia ladies.*

66 I simply ache from smiling. Why are women expected to beam all the time? It's unfair. If a man looks solemn, it's automatically assumed he's a serious person, not a miserable one. **99**

—QUEEN ELIZABETH II *of England, as entitled to the occasional* annus horribilus *as anyone.*

66 It is, I imagine, rather disturbing to see me eat a hard-boiled egg—I get the egg covered in lipstick, and my lower lip tends to fold down and swab my chin. . . . I don't even want to talk about what happens when I blow my nose. 99

—*Painted lady* ELIZABETH MCCRACKEN, *presumed to be a Jackson Pollock fan.*

66 I'll make some concessions if the request is reasonable. If someone tells me to comb my hair, I'll comb my hair. If someone tells me to dye it blond, they can go to hell. **99**

—*The darkly defiant* JANE WALLACE, *CBS correspondent.*

66 I wanted to be the first woman to burn her bra, but it would have taken the fire department four days to put it out. **99**

—*Flamboyant* DOLLY PARTON, *eye-catching even without bosoms* flambée.

66 I know I have a big bust, but I don't feel I'm any better than anyone who's had implants. **99**

—PATRICIA ARQUETTE, *an actress of admirable largesse.*

66 These puppies are mine and I love 'em. **99**

—*A newly bosomy* BRETT BUTLER. *For all we know, the happily implanted comedian is fond of her canine friends too.*

66 I am not an animal, so why should I wear a cage. **99**

—*Braless beauty* ANNA MAGNANI, *infamous for refusing to suppress her flesh . . . or her fits of offscreen rage.*

66 Who's gonna take me seriously with this on my head? **99**

—LEANZA CORNETT. *Though she balked at being crowned a beauty, Miss America 1993 finally conceded to carry her headgear in her hand.*

66 Nature gives you the face you have when you are twenty. Life shapes the face you have at thirty. But it is up to you to earn the face you have at fifty. 99

66 How many cares one loses when one decides not to be something, but to be someone. 99

66 Since everything is in our heads, we had better not lose them. 99

—*Couturier* GABRIELLE "COCO" CHANEL, *a very fashionable French revolutionary.*

66 In the gym, I only wear black and diamonds. **99**

> —*The sartorially astute* DONATELLA VERSACE. *No pearls while pumping iron, please.*

66 I resent the idea that you can't be both sexy and smart. When I dyed my hair, the peroxide didn't fry my brain cells. **99**

> —*Actress* LONI ANDERSON. *It's the color that's artificial, not the intelligence.*

66 I always wondered if *Little Women* would have done as well if Alcott had called it *Big Women*. **99**

—*Pulitzer Prize-winning playwright* WENDY WASSERSTEIN. *Size isn't everything . . . or is it?*

66 I feel more beautiful when I'm a little bit heavier. **99**

—*Actress* ANDIE MACDOWELL, *fully conscious of the cheesecake factor.*

❝ I'd like to be the first model who becomes a woman. **❞**

  —*Toothsome* LAUREN HUTTON, *good-looking despite (or because of) her gap.*

❝ Wake Up, I'm Fat! **❞**

  —*Pro-avoirdupois actress* CAMRYN MANHEIM, *who thusly titled her eye-opening off-Broadway show in 1996.*

66 You're not fat, you're in the wrong country. **99**

—*Plus-size model* DENISE WALKER, *an even bigger babe abroad.*

3.

*Pillow
Patter*

66 This relationship is sexual or it's nothing. **99**

> —*Prurient philosopher* AYN RAND. *Let Atlas shrug—at age fifty, randy Ayn demanded full attention from her favorite young acolyte.*

66 He always have orgasm and he doesn't wait for me to have an orgasm. He's selfish. I don't think it's fair so I pull back the sheets and then I did it. **99**

> —*Long-suffering spouse* LORENA BOBBITT, *who finally got her hubby's attention (or whatever) when she cut him off at the pass.*

66 I'm a bad woman, but I'm damn good company. **99**

—FANNY BRICE. *Though best known for her roles in Ziegfeld's Follies, funny Fanny also committed a few faux pas of her own.*

66 Glamour is just sex that got civilized. **99**

—*Sarong-clad siren* DOROTHY LAMOUR. *Fittingly, one of dishy Dottie's wrap-arounds wound up in the hoity-toity Smithsonian.*

66 Eros is the youngest of the gods. He is also the most tired. 99

66 To have or not to have, which is worse? 99

> —NATALIE BARNEY. *An American expatriate, the salacious salon-keeper was known in the early 1900s for making a mean cucumber sandwich, and also a famous French courtesan.*

66 Wear a taffeta slip that *who-o-shes* and *crackles* when you move. This makes men delirious. . . . Rub your thighs together when you walk. The *squish-squish* sound of nylon also has a frenzying effect. **99**

—*Creative* Cosmo *girls* GAEL GREENE *and* JEANNIE SAKEL, *revealing some startling techniques for having fun in (or with!) all your clothes.*

66 My great-grandmother had an affair with your great-grandfather. **99**

> —*The well-connected* CAMILLA PARKER-BOWLES, *who introduced herself to Prince Charles with this faintly incestuous, absolutely factual pick-up line. (Sorry to say, it's highly unlikely that Camilla's come-on will work for you or me.)*

66 I have often remarked to my husband that we might have had more children if we had taken more vacations. **99**

> —HILLARY CLINTON, *wife of the 42nd president of the United States; mother of one.*

66 There are always more than two choices. Always. Always. Always. **99**

> —*Top pornographer* PAT CALIFIA, *who suggests that you park your PC principles outside the bedroom door.*

66 Oh, you mean I'm homosexual! Of course I am, and heterosexual too. But what's that got to do with my headache? **99**

> —*Famed meter maid* EDNA ST. VINCENT MILLAY, *whose doctor held that love between ladies led to malaise.*

66 I'm not really in touch with the male side of myself. But it's fun to play a drag queen. **99**

—*"Victor/Victoria" stand-in* LIZA MINNELLI, *a happy camp-er at last.*

66 I don't want to be touched by people I don't know. I have that right. **99**

—*Pseudo-lifeguard* PAMELA LEE, *who successfully reneged on a contract calling for her to demo an entirely different set of strokes.*

66 The mammary fixation is the most infantile—and most American—of the sex fetishes. 99

> —Movie critic MOLLY HASKELL, *one woman you'll never see in (or out of) a Wonderbra.*

66 Oh, plenty of times. Are you kidding—who hasn't? We're Americans. 99

> —Licensed driver HOLLY HUNTER, *in response to an exceedingly rude query (but hey—we're Americans!) concerning her autoerotic experiences.*

66 Interference with self-pleasure is a very bad thing for children. **99**

—MARY CALDERONE. *The planned parenthood pioneer who founded SIECUS (Sex Information and Education Council of the United States) in 1961 made less liberal citizens SICK.*

66 I have an inalienable constitutional and natural right to love whom I may, to love as long or as short a period as I can, to change that love every day if I please! **99**

—VICTORIA WOODHULL, *who campaigned for this country's top office in 1872 on a platform that included free love and communism. Students of history may recall that Ulysses S. Grant was not forced to vacate the White House as a result.*

" Yep, I'm gay. **"**

—ELLEN DEGENERES, *TV's only self-outing sitcom star.*

" What woman doesn't spend 90 percent of her life going in and out of the closet? **"**

—*Designer* DONNA KARAN, *not at all discombobulated by the disclosure of Ellen's supposedly stylish sexual preference.*

66 Homosexuals make the best friends because they care about you as a woman and are not jealous. They love you but don't try to screw up your head. **99**

> —*Reformed jet-setter* BIANCA JAGGER, *who would like you to know that some of her best friends are gay.*

66 I can play a heterosexual. I know how they walk. I know how they talk. You don't have to be one to play one. **99**

> — *The multi-talented* LILY TOMLIN, *a straight woman when her profession demands it.*

66 Wouldn't it be great if you could only get AIDS from giving money to television preachers? **99**

> —ELAYNE BOOSLER, *a stand-up comedian who stands* for *something.*

66 The last time I had sex with men, we were demonstrating against Nixon by day, eating psychedelic mushrooms by night, and fucking in between. No one I knew went out on 'dates.' I had no feeling for contemporary heterosexual courtship. 99

—SUSIE BRIGHT. *On the other hand, the audacious author of* Susie Sexpert's Lesbian Sex World *has Sapphic seduction down pat.*

66 My lesbianism is an act of Christian charity. All those women out there are praying for a man, and I'm giving them my share. **99**

66 The only queer people are those who don't love anybody. **99**

66 An army of lovers shall not fail. **99**

> —*Writer* RITA MAE BROWN: *gay as all get-out, and sometimes downright giddy.*

66 I have met many feminists who were not Lesbians—but I have never met a Lesbian who was not a feminist. **99**

> —*Socially-active author* MARTHA SHELLEY, *wise in the ways of (at least two kinds of) women.*

66 Women who assume authority are unnatural. Unnatural women are lesbians. Therefore all the leaders of the women's movement were presumed to be lesbians. **99**

> —*Humorist* JANE O'REILLY, *the odd libber who happens to be (stop me if you've heard this one before) happily heterosexual.*

66 All the lesbians are starting to fuck men. All the straight girls want to be lesbians. I'm feeling very alone. **99**

—*Chanteuse* kd lang, *a distinctly unlikely cross-over artist.*

66 All women are lesbians except those who don't know it. **99**

—JILL JOHNSTON, *renowned radical—and one humdinger of an optimistic dyke.*

66 I could never hang from a chandelier. **99**

    —Hollywoodite HEATHER LOCKLEAR, *who obviously never even tried to light up her ex's life in the manner so shrewishly suggested by her successor.*

66 If I wanted everyone to know who I'm sleeping with, I'd put my bed in the street. **99**

    —Secretive supermodel VERONICA WEBB. *Check her out on the catwalk, not in the crosswalk.*

66 You could put a bag over a guy's head and have the best orgasm of your life, but so what? **99**

—*Dictatorial* DR. LAURA *(Schlessinger), America's least touchy-feely shrink.*

4.

$\mathcal{S}$tormy
$\mathcal{R}$eformers

" You'll be free or die. **"**

> —HARRIET TUBMAN. *Timorous Underground Railway passengers toughened up quick when Tubman brandished her revolver.*

" You have put me in here a cub, but I will come out roaring like a lion, and I will make all hell howl! **"**

> —*Temperamental temperance crusader* CARRY NATION, *utterly unsubdued by her stint in the slammer.*

❝ I am what you call a hooligan! **❞**

—EMMELINE PANKHURST, *England's most insufferable suffragette.*

❝ A gentleman opposed to their enfranchisement once said to me, 'Women have never produced anything of any value to the world.' I told him the chief product of the women had been the men, and left it to him to decide whether the product was of any value. **❞**

—ANNA SHAW, *the mouthiest minister this side of the Mississippi (or, for that matter, the other one).*

66 We first crush people to the earth, and then claim the right of trampling on them forever, because they are prostrate. **99**

>   —*Abolitionist* LYDIA MARIA CHILD, *banned in white-bred Boston in the early 1800s.*

66 We can bear with great philosophy the sufferings of others, especially if we do not actually see them. **99**

>   —ALBION FELLOWS BACON, *a rather cynical turn-of-the-century social worker.*

66 In a world where there is so much to be done, I felt strongly impressed that there must be something for me to do. **99**

> —*Do-gooder* DOROTHEA DIX, *who founded thirty-two mental hospitals in her spare time. Other aspiring angels of mercy, however, didn't pass muster with dour Dorothea, Chief of the Union Army Nursing Corps, unless they were plain, proper, and past the age of thirty.*

66 No matter the fight, don't be ladylike! God almighty made women and the Rockefeller gang of thieves made the ladies. **99**

66 Injustice boils in men's hearts as does steel in its caldron, ready to pour forth, white hot, in the fullness of time. **99**

66 Get it right, I ain't a humanitarian ... I'm a hell-raiser! **99**

—*Militant labor organizer Mary* "MOTHER" JONES, *one mean maternal unit to mess with.*

66 I used to be radical and vindictive. I am still radical, but I am not vindictive. Time has mellowed me. **99**

    —*Reformed reformist* MARY ELIZABETH LEASE, the *People's Party girl of the late 1800s.*

66 I am prepared to sacrifice every so-called privilege I possess in order to have a few rights. **99**

    —*Vassar girl* INEZ MILHOLLAND, *who staged a wild women's rights rally. . . in 1909.*

66 Why should we pay taxes when we have no part in the honours, the commands, the statecraft, for which you contend against each other with such harmful results? **99**

    —Irate orator HORTENSIA, *circa 50* BC. *Headstrong H got her toga in a tangle when Roman leaders extracted a tax from females only . . . to fund a civil war.*

66 The older I get, the greater power I seem to have to help the world; I am like a snowball—the further I am rolled the more I gain. **99**

66 Those who are really in earnest must be willing to be anything or nothing in the world's estimation. **99**

66 Failure is impossible. **99**

—SUSAN B. ANTHONY, *the formidable founding mother of 19th-century American feminism.*

66 While it was disagreeable and unreasonable to have our wearing apparel described in the papers, it was inevitable in this stage of woman's progress, editors and reporters being much more able to judge of our clothes than they were of our arguments. **99**

—*Suffragist* OLYMPIA BROWN, *whose pointed observation appeared in print—no, not yesterday, but nearly ninety years ago.*

❝ We couldn't possibly know where it would lead, but we knew it had to be done. **❞**

> —*Faith-full* BETTY FRIEDAN, *the big mama who blew the whistle on the feminine mystique.*

66 When I was in high school, I wanted to be a cheerleader and be popular and have a guy with a car who could dance. And probably if I'd been able to be a cheerleader, I wouldn't have to grow up to be president of NOW, but I was too clumsy, I couldn't get my hands and feet to cooperate. **99**

—PATRICIA IRELAND, *a die-hard feminist by default.*

66 Don't agonize. Organize. **99**

66 The biggest sin is sitting on your ass. **99**

66 If it's a movement, I sometimes think it needs a laxative. **99**

> —*Fleet-tongued* FLORYNCE KENNEDY. *Fortunately, the Ür-activist of the Sixties and Seventies seldom stayed down in the dumps for long.*

66 Just think—guns have a constitutional amendment protecting them and women don't. **99**

—*Hotshot* ELEANOR SMEAL, *president of NOW from 1977 to 1987.*

66 Sperm Are People Too! **99**

—*Tongue-in-cheek motto of "Ladies Against Women," the pro-choice coalition founded by feminists with (we swear on our holy Birkenstocks) a sense of humor.*

66 If women want any rights more than they have, why don't they just take them, and not be talking about it. **99**

—*Abolitionist orator* SOJOURNER TRUTH. *Seize the day, ladies—or shut the hell up!*

5.

Leery
Lovers

66 You bitch, leave my husband alone! **99**

> —*Trophy wife* IVANA TRUMP, *who tangled with incipient trophy wife Marla Maples on the touchy topic of The(ir) Donald.*

66 I thought he was nuts or something. **99**

> —*Prescient* PAT NIXON, *discussing the peculiar courtship style of the man she eventually wed. (Decidedly a dark horse candidate, Tricky Dick drove his elusive love object to and from her dates with other men.)*

" Love is like playing checkers. You have to know which man to move. **"**

> —JACKIE "MOMS" MABLEY. *A Mom, but not a Mabley, at the outset of her career, the Apollo theater legend lifted her last name from Beau #1, who owed her for certain favors.*

" I shot him 'cause I love him, God damn him! **"**

> —MADAM TESSIE WALL. *Marriage counseling not being the mode in 1917, the San Francisco procuress simply took a therapeutic potshot at the man who done her wrong.*

66 I know what I wish Ralph Nader would investigate next. Marriage. It's not safe—it's not safe at all. 99

> —Playwright JEAN KERR, *whose stock-in-trade (professionally speaking, anyway) was* liaisons dangereuse.

66 I never believed marriage was a lasting institution. . . . I thought that to be married for five years was to be married forever. 99

> —Love interest LAUREN BACALL, *who endured an eternity of wedded bliss (well, okay, twelve years) with Bogie until death did them part.*

66 Love *is* everything it's cracked up to be. That's why people are so cynical about it. **99**

66 No one has ever found wisdom without also being a fool. **99**

66 Men and women, women and men. It will never work. **99**

—*Erotic novelist* ERICA JONG, *a fearless frequent flyer.*

66 I know a lot of people didn't expect our relationship to last—but we've just celebrated our two months anniversary. 99

>—*Actress* BRITT EKLAND, *thinking fast.*

66 Any woman who accepts aloneness as the natural by-product of success is accepting the punishment for a crime she didn't commit. 99

>—MARLO THOMAS, *perfectly partnered by Phil Donahue despite her status as a Sixties sitcom phenom.*

66 Jealousy is the fear of losing the thing you love most. It's very normal. Suspicion is the thing that's abnormal. 99

—JERRY HALL, *the model Mrs. for monogamy-challenged Mick.*

66 In Hollywood, all marriages are happy. It's trying to live together afterwards that causes all the problems. 99

—*Actress* SHELLEY WINTERS. *As the wife of three, she earned her cynicism the old-fashioned way.*

66 Jealousy is not a barometer by which the depth of love can be read. It merely records the degree of the lover's insecurity. 99

66 To make love the requirement of a lifelong marriage is exceedingly difficult, and only a few people can achieve it. I don't believe in setting universal standards that a large proportion of people can't reach. 99

—MARGARET MEAD. *Her knowledge of human nature notwithstanding, the eminent anthropologist failed to achieve enduring amour . . . three times in a row.*

❝ I believe in large families; every woman should have at least three husbands. **❞**

> —*Entertainer* ZSA ZSA GABOR. *No hypocrite, she, glamorous Gabor set up housekeeping with eight different guys (though not, of course, simultaneously).*

❝ I am trying for nothing so hard in my own personal life as how not to be respectable when married. **❞**

> —*Leftist labor writer* MARY HEATON VORSE. *Three bouts of matrimony didn't mellow the bohemian bride, who went on to serve as the oldest US news correspondent during World War II.*

66 Love is moral even without legal marriage, but marriage is immoral without love. 99

66 All vows binding forever the life of feeling are a violence of one's personality, since one cannot be held accountable for the transformation of one's feeling. 99

—ELLEN KEY, *professional provocateur. Not surprisingly, her ultra-Swedish social theories had many of her 19th-century contemporaries sweating in their saunas.*

66 A real marriage. . . . is two lovers who live together. A priest may well say certain words, a notary may well sign certain papers— I regard these preparations in the same way that a lover regards the rope ladder that he ties to his mistress's window. 99

66 I will not be cheated—nor will I employ long years of repentance for moments of joy. 99

66 Nature is seldom in the wrong, custom always. 99

—LADY MARY WORTLEY MONTAGU. *Though she shocked her peers by bedding extramarital beaux, lusty Lady M also introduced the smallpox vaccine to England, saving countless of her countrymen's lives.*

66 Love is only the dessert of life. The minute you try to live on dessert, you get sick of it, and you can get sicker of love than you can of anything else in the world. 99

66 The reason that husbands and wives do not understand each other is because they belong to different sexes. 99

> —DOROTHY DIX, *the down-to-earth "Dear Abby" of her (turn-of-the-century) day.*

66 If there is to be any romance in marriage woman must be given every chance to earn a decent living at other occupations. Otherwise no man can be sure that he is loved for himself alone, and that his wife did not come to the Registry Office because she had no luck at the Labour Exchange. **99**

—*Journalist* Rebecca West. *Known for her wit(s), the radical Brit never did wed writer HG Wells, the man who made her a mother.*

66 I'd like to get married because I like the idea of a man being required by law to sleep with me every night. 99

66 Why get married and make one man miserable when I can stay single and make thousands miserable. 99

—*Quipster* CARRIE SNOW, *as schizoid as any other single on the subject of tying the knot.*

" Mr. Right's coming, but he's in Africa, and he's walking! **"**

—*Guardedly-optimistic* OPRAH WINFREY, *the most watched woman in America.*

" It's a big, round, honking diamond! **"**

—BROOKE SHIELDS, *as a blushing (or so we would certainly hope) bride-to-be.*

6.

Professional Confessional

66 I got my start by giving myself a start. **99**

> —*Make-up maven* MADAME CJ WALKER. *And as we all know (or should), black beauty care made Madame a millionaire.*

66 Be a leper missionary! **99**

> —*Such was the motherly advice doled out by* DIANE LADD, *who emphatically did not wish daughter Laura Dern to follow in her footsteps as an actress.*

66 There is nothing that makes me feel more alive than making money. **99**

> —*The Big Apple's ubiquitous* BROOKE ASTOR. *In later years, of course, the grande dame of good causes got her kicks from distributing the cash.*

66 The whole government is afraid of me, and well they may be. **99**

> —*Nosy newswoman* ANNE ROYALL, *convicted in 1829 of an entirely sex-specific crime: being a "common scold."*

66 Rage is to writers what water is to fish. A laid-back writer is like an orgasmic prostitute—an anomaly. 99

—NIKKI GIOVANNI, *impassioned poet.*

66 I'm so sick of Nancy Drew I could vomit. 99

—MILDRED BENSON, *who parlayed the character of an excessively perky teen sleuth into an entire literary career. (Wisely, Benson published her stomach-turning series under a pseudonym.)*

66 I always thought of photography as a naughty thing to do—that was one of my favorite things about it, and when I first did it, I felt very perverse. 99

> —DIANE ARBUS, *whose shocking portraits of the physically peculiar not only flirted with voyeurism, but often consummated the affair.*

66 My mother told me, 'Never call boys on the telephone. Let them take the first step.' If I'd done that, I'd probably be somebody's secretary right now instead of secretary of state. 99

> —*Rhode Island politician* SUSAN FARMER, *not destined to do Windows for a living.*

66 Of course my father always said I should have been a boy. He said, Don't grow up to be a woman, and what he meant by that was, a housewife. **99**

—MARIA GOEPPERT MAYER. *Unable to alter her anatomy, Mayer nonetheless pocketed the second Nobel Prize in physics awarded to a woman (Marie Curie snared the first) in 1963.*

❝ I always believed that if you set out to be successful, then you already were. **❞**

> —KATHERINE DUNHAM, *Doctor of Anthropology. On her toes in more ways than one, the scholar in ballet slippers founded one of America's most-acclaimed black dance troupes in 1939.*

❝ Genius only means an infinite capacity for taking pains. **❞**

> —*Social reformer* JANE ELLICE HOPKINS. *Like Thomas Edison (her peer across The Pond), hard-working Hopkins swore by perspiration, not inspiration.*

66 I may be kindly, I am ordinarily gentle, but in my line of business I am obliged to will terribly what I will at all. 99

 —EMPRESS CATHERINE II *of Russia, whose job description seems to have included savaging Poland, ravaging Turkey, and possibly performing unspeakable acts with a horse.*

66 People have told me ninety-nine things that I had to do as First Lady, and I haven't done one of them. 99

 —JACQUELINE KENNEDY. *When the quirky Queen of Camelot skipped a shindig in her honor, the president of the US was forced to take her place.*

66 There's only one woman I know who could never be a symphony conductor, and that's the Venus de Milo. **99**

> —*The armed and dangerous* Margaret Hillis, *former director of the Chicago Symphony Orchestra.*

66 Talent is like electricity. We don't understand electricity. We use it. **99**

> —Maya Angelou, *shockingly prolific author/activist.*

66 When I think about my life, I am sure I will not arrive at an old age. But I would rather sing one day as a lion than a hundred years as a sheep. **99**

—CECELIA BARTOLI, *Italy's most macha mezzosoprano.*

66 The thing to do [for insomnia] is to get an opera score and read *that*. That will bore you to death. **99**

—*Vocal virtuoso* MARILYN HORNE, *who evidently doesn't log a lot of late-night overtime.*

❝ I did this picture. I did that picture. I went skiing. Then I did another picture. Then I went swimming. And I was happily married. Who gives a damn? **❞**

> —CLAUDETTE COLBERT. *Actually, the conjugally-content actress never resided with Spouse Number One and seldom mentioned her work (which comprised some sixty-four films) to Number Two. Not, we hasten to add, that it's any of our business.*

66 Librarians like to be given trouble; they exist for it, they are geared to it. For the location of a mislaid volume, an uncatalogued item, your good librarian has a ferret's nose. Give her a scent and she jumps the leash, her eye bright with battle. 99

—CATHERINE DRINKER BOWEN. *As a professional biographer, CDB had ample opportunity to observe the ladies who say "Shhh" in their native habitat.*

66 Food faddists and crackpots. . . . seem to believe that unless food tastes like Socratic hemlock, it cannot build health. Frankly, I often wonder what such persons plan to do with good health in case they acquire it. **99**

—ADELLE DAVIS. *Far from a fanatic, the natural foods guru of the Sixties and Seventies once created quite a stir by sipping a Coke in an airport.*

66 Too many cooks may spoil the broth, but it only takes one to burn it. **99**

> —*Chef* JULIA CHILD, *the quirky queen of TV cuisine.*

66 In many ways writing is the act of saying *I,* of imposing oneself upon other people, of saying *listen to me, see it my way, change your mind.* It's an aggressive, even hostile act. **99**

> —JOAN DIDION, *wrathful writer.*

66 I began quite early in life to sense the thrill a girl attains in supplying money to a man. 99

—ANITA LOOS. *The solvent satirist behind* Gentlemen Prefer Blondes, *Loos preferred to bring home the bacon.*

66 Show me a person who has never made a mistake and I'll show you somebody who has never achieved much. 99

—*Glamour girl* JOAN COLLINS. *The perennial vixen courted disaster in fifty B movies before "Dynasty" made her a middle-aged mega-star.*

66 I'd rather risk an ugly surprise than rely on things I know I can do. 99

—Abstract artist HELEN FRANKENTHALER. An atypical femme of the Fifties, Frankenthaler perfected her trademark "stain and soak" technique in the studio, not the laundry room.

66 Dreck is dreck and no amount of fancy polish is going to make it anything else. 99

—TV vet LINDA ELLERBEE. Unlike her manicured peers, the noted anti-schlock jock refused to "act and model the news."

66 Fortunately analysis is not the only way to resolve inner conflicts. Life itself still remains a very effective therapist. **99**

66 Concern should drive us into action and not into a depression. **99**

—*Heretical headshrinker* KAREN HORNEY, *apparently bent on talking herself out of a job.*

66 I am a woman who enjoys herself very much; sometimes I lose, sometimes I win. **99**

　　—MATA HARI. *True to her philosophy, World War I's seductive double agent went out with a bang.*

66 I hate money when it is not my own. **99**

　　—FRANCES BROOKE. *Though the playwright's name carried a certain weight in 18th-century London, she was seldom plagued by extra pounds.*

" I had a 'real' job for seven months. My soul fell asleep. **"**

—*Sculptor* BARBRO HEDSTROM, *not cut out for a conventional life.*

" Work don't kill nobody. It make you tired though. **"**

—*Folk artist* CLEMENTINE HUNTER, *Louisiana's answer to Grandma Moses. Fully entitled to her fatigue, hardworking Hunter produced more than 5,000 paintings during her second fifty years of life.*

7.

$\mathcal{C}$ro-Magnon
$\mathcal{C}$ritique

66 I have never wanted to be a man. I have often wanted to be effective as a woman but I never thought that trousers would do the trick. **99**

> —ELEANOR ROOSEVELT. *The domestically indifferent first lady was content to let FDR wear the pants . . . but she certainly didn't plan to iron them.*

66 I've been a man many times. That's what I'm trying to atone for now. **99**

> —HELEN *"I Am Woman"* REDDY—*this time around, anyway.*

66 I don't want a dick even for one day. **99**

—*Conceptualist* JENNY HOLZER, *applauded for her bold experiments in the artistic forum, not the anatomical one.*

66 If that's the world's smartest man, God help us. **99**

—LUCILLE FEYNMAN, *from whose skeptical genes sprang a son once touted as the greatest genius on the globe (though perhaps not the most likely to wash behind his ears).*

66 I am more and more convinced that man is a dangerous creature. 99

66 No man ever prospered in the world without the consent and cooperation of his wife. 99

—ABIGAIL ADAMS. *A tad too ahead of her time for comfort, controversial First Lady #2 apparently aspired to the title of Superfeminist #1.*

66 The only way to get along is to seek the difficult job, always do it well, and see that you get paid for it properly. Oh, yes, and don't forget to exploit men all you can. Because if you don't they will exploit you. **99**

—EL DORADO JONES, *inventor and entrepreneur. Jaded with regard to gender relations, Jones maintained an entirely man-free factory in the early 1900s.*

66 Freud is the father of psychoanalysis. It has no mother. 99

66 Probably the only place where a man can feel really secure is in a maximum security prison, except for the imminent threat of release. 99

66 Is it too much to ask that a woman be spared the daily struggle for superhuman beauty in order to offer it to the caresses of a subhumanly ugly mate? 99

—*Anti-social critic* GERMAINE GREER, *dedicated to the proposition that there's nothing pretty about patriarchy.*

66 I believe that if a man does a job as well as a woman, he should be paid as much. 99

—*Sly* CELESTE HOLM, *an irony-enriched entertainer.*

66 Beware of men who cry. It's true that men who cry are sensitive to and in touch with feelings, but the only feelings they tend to be sensitive to and in touch with are their own. 99

—NORA EPHRON, *embittered ex-wife. And indeed, her hubby-bashing* Heartburn *was enough to make a grown man bawl.*

66 The first time you buy a house you think how pretty it is and sign the check. The second time you look to see if the basement has termites. It's the same with men. 99

—*Love-shy* LUPE VELEZ, *infamous in the 1930s for lounging about film sets minus her lingerie.*

66 Some people hurl themselves in front of a train. I hurled myself in front of another white man. **99**

> —DOROTHY DANDRIDGE. *Though dazzling Dorothy made the cover of* Life *in 1954, Hollywood never did figure out what to do with a leading lady who wasn't lily white.*

66 It's odd that men feel they must protect women, since for the most part they must be protected from men. **99**

> —ABIGAIL DUNIWAY. *A pioneer feminist (as well as a pioneer, period) in the Wild West, Duniway was capable of taking care of herself, thank you just the same.*

66 I myself find it much less difficult to strangle a man than to fear him. **99**

—QUEEN CHRISTINA, *Sweden's single-minded sovereign from 1632 to 1654.*

66 All I wanted was a man with a single heart and we would stay together as our hair turned white, not somebody always after wriggling fish with his big bamboo rod. **99**

—*Peeved poet* CHUO WEN-CHUN. *Evidently fly fishing was a favorite male pastime in ancient China too.*

66 Seduction is often difficult to distinguish from rape. In seduction, the rapist bothers to buy a bottle of wine. 99

—*Activist* ANDREA DWORKIN, *notorious for her polarized position on intercourse.*

66 They [men] always want to put their things in. That's all they want. 99

—*Movie legend* MARLENE DIETRICH, *who reportedly favored a different form of gratification—and perhaps a different gender as well.*

66 When genetic control is possible—and it soon will be—it goes without saying that we should produce only whole, complete beings, not physical defects or deficiencies, including emotional deficiencies, such as maleness. 99

—*Sixties separatist* VALERIE SOLANAS. *After attempting to off Andy Warhol, the agitated anarchist expressed her sincere regret . . . that she hadn't done more target practice.*

66 It seldom happens, I think, that a man has the civility to die when all the world wishes it. **99**

—MARIE DE SÉVIGNÉ. *Yet another compulsive correspondent of the 17th century, droll de Sévigné never published a word . . . but made a career out of composing letters. (Her daughter, who received nearly one thousand of mama's missives, may have made a career out of reading them.)*

❝ The more I see of men, the more I like dogs. **❞**

> —CLARA BOW, *randy vamp of the Roaring Twenties. Rumor had it that the sex-obsessed starlet "laid everything but the linoleum"—including the entire University of Southern California football team.*

❝ Without such men, 'this book would not have been possible.' On the other hand, it would not have been necessary. **❞**

> —*Radical* ROBIN MORGAN, *who thusly acknowledged the special contributions of three penised persons (one of whom happened to be her spouse) to the 1970 anthology* Sisterhood is Powerful.

8.

Glib
Libbers

66 If you have a vagina and a point of view, that's a deadly combination. 99

> —*Actress* SHARON STONE, *famous for flaunting both.*

66 A hole is not destiny. A protuberance is not destiny. If anatomy were destiny, the wheel could not have been invented: we would have been limited by legs. 99

> —*Cultural critic* CYNTHIA OZICK, *pointing out the phallusy of the whole Freudian . . . thing.*

66 I'd much rather be a woman than a man. Women can cry, they can wear cute clothes, and they're first to be rescued off sinking ships. **99**

> —GILDA RADNER. *The odd "Saturday Night Live" regular who wasn't a guy, gifted Gilda had a rather retro rationale for the superiority of her sex.*

66 Women never have young minds. They are born three thousand years old. **99**

> —*Salt-of-the-earth dramatist* SHELAGH DELANEY, *who authored her acclaimed "A Taste of Honey" at the approximate age of 3018.*

66 One is not born a woman, one becomes one. 99

66 A man would never get the notion of writing a book on the peculiar situation of the human male. 99

66 All oppression creates a state of war. 99

> —SIMONE DE BEAUVOIR, *Sartre's bosom buddy. As students of social theory will recall, ladies did not come first in her seminal* Second Sex.

66 The right Education of the Female Sex, as it is in a manner everywhere neglected, so it ought to be generally lamented. Most in this depraved later Age think a Woman learned and wise enough if she can distinguish her Husbands Bed from anothers. **99**

—HANNAH WOOLLEY. *Seldom, we suspect, has anyone advanced a racier argument for equal access to the three Rs than housemaid Hannah, who flourished (or at least held forth) in the late 1600s.*

66 Women are systematically degraded by receiving the trivial attentions which men think it manly to pay to the sex, when, in fact, men are insultingly supporting their own superiority. **99**

66 I do not wish [women] to have power over men, but over themselves. **99**

66 It is justice, not charity, that is wanting in the world. **99**

—*Writer* MARY WOLLSTONECRAFT. *The scourge of 18th-century sexists didn't feel that fellows should have all the fun—or, for that matter, all the funds.*

66 Women are repeatedly accused of taking things personally. I cannot see any other honest way of taking them. **99**

—MARYA MANNES. *What the thrice-divorced author/artist/WWII intelligence analyst* couldn't *see herself taking: male chauvinist manure . . . from anyone.*

66 Before devising any blueprint that includes the assumption of Having It All, we need to ask . . . Why do we need Everything? **99**

—LETTY COTTIN POGREBIN, *radical feminist refuse-nik.*

66 Male supremacy has kept woman down. It has not knocked her out. 99

66 Fifty years [Freud] spends analyzing women. And he still can't find out what they want. So this makes him the world's greatest expert on female psychology? 99

> —CLARE BOOTH LUCE. *Not even the Pope could meet the exacting standards of the prickly playwright (and diplomat and journalist and politician) who penned "The Women" in 1936. "But, Madam, I am Catholic," the pontiff supposedly protested when Clare finally cornered him in the Vatican.*

66 Those nuts that burn their bras and walk around all disheveled and hate men? They're crazy. Crazy. 99

66 Women's Liberation is just a lot of foolishness. It's the men who are discriminated against. They can't bear children. And no one's likely to do anything about that. 99

—GOLDA MEIR, *just another working mother.*

66 The real butches are straight. 99

66 Leaving sex to the feminists is like letting your dog vacation at the taxidermist's. 99

66 The motto of my feminism is: *Deal with it*. We cannot have a society where we are constantly running to other people to complain. 99

—*From the orifice of* CAMILLE PAGLIA, *contentious PhD.*

66 There are staunch, political, angry women, who are like 'Don't you see the value we have, fuckers?', and then there are women who get their tits done. Both are trying to prove something to men. For me, feminism is somewhere between the bimbos and the ballbusters. 99

—LAURA DERN, *a profoundly (and profanely) middle-of-the-road movie star.*

66 Among poor people, there's not any question about women being strong—even stronger than men—they work in the fields right along with the men. When your survival is at stake, you don't have these questions about yourself like middle-class women do. **99**

—DOLORES HUERTA. *Co-founder of the United Farm Workers, the Chicana labor leader wasn't sidelined by her sex or her race—or even her youthful allegiance to the Republican Party.*

66 The roosters may crow, but the hens deliver the goods. **99**

> —ANN RICHARDS, *the gal who governed the great agricultural state of Texas from 1991 to 1995.*

66 Work by a male writer is often spoken of by critics admiring it as having 'balls;' ever hear anyone speak admiringly of work by a woman as having 'tits'? **99**

> —MARGARET ATWOOD, *one of North America's best-endowed novelists.*

" Genius has no sex! "

> —GERMAINE DE STAËL, *who had a lot of both. (At the moment, however, the saucy salon hostess was simply trying to score an audience with a nude Napoleon.)*

9.

Voluble Venuses

66 I am a harlot and I intend to remain a harlot. **99**

> —*France's upfront* THÉRÈSE LACHMANN, *circa 1850. And indeed, she was, and did.*

66 You are what you *dare!* **99**

> —*Eternally X-perimenting* XAVIERA HOLLANDER—*everything a woman (or at least a "Happy Hooker") could hope to be.*

66 I wasn't really naked. I simply didn't have any clothes on. **99**

> —JOSEPHINE BAKER. *The toast of Paris in the 1920s, the daring (or perhaps merely hungry) dancer liked to strut her stuff in a G-string fashioned from bananas.*

66 I did not find the business all that disgusting. You pick your customers, you meet interesting people and youth is not a prerequisite. **99**

> —MARGO ST. JAMES, *enthusiastic entrepreneur, on the many perks of going pro.*

66 My father warned me about men and booze, but he never mentioned a *word* about women and cocaine. 99

66 Nobody can be exactly like me. Sometimes even I have trouble doing it. 99

66 If I had my life to live again, I'd make the same mistakes, only sooner. 99

—TALLULAH BANKHEAD. *Bold, beautiful, and flagrantly bisexual, the boastful bad girl of American theater kissed and told—and told, and told, and told.*

66 I think if a woman has a right to an abortion and to control her body, then she has the right to exploit her body and make money from it. We have it hard enough. Why give up one of our major assets? **99**

—*Penthouse Corporation president* KATHY KEETON. *No nudes was obviously bad nudes in her (we see now) flawlessly feminist book.*

66 I was a prostitute for three months before I realized it. The job was so much fun and I liked it so much, that I couldn't imagine it was prostitution. 99

66 Sex [can] cure an asthma attack. I saved a man's life once. 99

66 Have you ever noticed how very different everyone's tongue is? I have. 99

—*Former B-girl* ANNIE SPRINKLE, *an exceptionally ebullient bawdy worker.*

66 If I could be the 'condom queen' and get every young person who engaged in sex to use a condom in the United States, I would wear a crown on my head with a condom on it! I would! **99**

> —JOCELYN ELDERS. *Promoting safe sex proved risky business for the former Surgeon General, booted from her bully pulpit in 1994 when it became clear she might also serve as masturbation monarch.*

66 Maybe I'll make a 'Mary Poppins' movie and shove the umbrella up my ass. **99**

> —*Porn phenomenon* MARILYN CHAMBERS, *constitutionally incapable of going PG.*

66 Men are more often defeated because of their own clumsiness than because of a woman's virtue. **99**

66 One needs a hundred times more esprit in order to love properly than to command armies. **99**

> —*17th-century courtesan* NINON DE LENCLOS, *whose great gift to her fellow Frenchwomen was teaching young nobles how to make nooky nicely.*

66 It's not true I had nothing on. I had the radio on. 99

66 I don't want to make money. I just want to be wonderful. 99

66 To put it bluntly, I seem to be a whole superstructure with no foundation. But I'm working on the foundation. 99

—*Mesmerizing* MARILYN MONROE, *the blonde that gentlemen of the pre-anorexic era preferred.*

66 So you are in love with me? Say it straight out, it is much more simple. **99**

> —MARIE DUPLESSIS, *a very popular Parisian, circa 1844. In Marie's line of work, it turns out, it was also more simple if she got the money up front.*

66 I'm the best damn cocksucker in Chicago and I've got the diamonds to prove it. **99**

> —*Mobster's moll* VIRGINIA HILL. *The few guys she didn't go for got the message when she flushed their tributes down the toilet.*

66 Romance without finance is a nuisance. 99

66 I at least chose a sin that's made quite a few people happier than they were before they met me. 99

—SALLY STANFORD. *Headmistress of the so-called "Stanford School of Advanced Studies" during World War II, Madam Sally assigned each "pupil" a personal tutor—or as many as he could afford.*

66 I only put clothes on so that I'm not naked when I go out shopping. **99**

66 When you act with your clothes on, it's a performance. When you act with your clothes off, it's a documentary. I don't do documentaries. **99**

66 Why do we all have to be naked to get along? **99**

—The trés jolie JULIA ROBERTS*—not a one-man woman, not a one-mood nude.*

66 When I can't sleep, I don't count sheep, I count lovers. And by the time I reach thirty-eight or thirty-nine, I'm asleep. **99**

—MIRIAM HOPKINS. *Though the frisky thespian once tried to lure Bette Davis into her boudoir, her usual policy was "no animals in bed."*

66 When I die, my epitaph should read: *She Paid the Bills*. That's the story of my private life. **99**

—*Box-office beauty* GLORIA SWANSON, *on the money but off the mark. (True enough—her financial affairs were in order.)*

66 I'm the girl who lost her reputation and never missed it. 99

66 The best way to hold a man is in your arms. 99

66 When I'm good I'm very good, but when I'm bad I'm better. 99

—MAE WEST, *one sex goddess who called (and directed) her own shots.*

66 You can't think with your clothes on. **99**

—The totally focused FLORENCE ALLEN. *A fascinating figure in the modern art world, palette-pleasing Flo posed unclothed for more than fifty years.*

66 I've always said: 'I'm happy to take my clothes off if the man takes his off. If you're willing to let him run around with his willy hanging out, I'm perfectly happy to run around in the buff.' But nobody ever makes that deal with me. **99**

—Potential nudist MICHELLE PFEIFFER.

66 The world thinks of me as such a scarlet woman; I'm almost purple. **99**

66 What do you expect me to do? Sleep alone? **99**

—*Gregarious* ELIZABETH TAYLOR, *seven times a bride.*

10.

*B*itchin'
*P*oliticians

" There's nothing wrong with America—except those jerks in Washington who're trying to run it! **"**

— MARTHA MITCHELL. *The favorite telephone freak of the Sixties media, motor-mouth Martha really had Richard ("I Am Not a Crook") Nixon's number.*

" A ship in port is safe, but that is not what ships are built for. **"**

— BENAZIR BHUTTO, *formerly both a Pakistani prisoner of state and her country's Prime Minister.*

66 Standing in the middle of the road is very dangerous; you get knocked down by traffic from both sides. **99**

> —*"Iron Maiden"* MARGARET THATCHER, *England's unswervingly Conservative PM.*

66 Authority without wisdom is like a heavy axe without an edge, fitter to bruise than polish. **99**

> —ANNE BRADSTREET. *Too through with fellows who found her "sex void of reason," America's first published poet noted that misogyny meant "treason" in Elizabethan England.*

66 True emancipation begins neither at the polls nor in courts. It begins in woman's soul. **99**

66 The most unpardonable sin in society is independence of thought. **99**

66 No real social change has ever come about without a revolution. **99**

—*Anarchist* EMMA GOLDMAN, *one of America's most disobedient civilians.*

66 To gain that which is worth having, it may be necessary to lose everything else. **99**

> —*North Ireland's irascible* BERNADETTE DEVLIN, *the most youthful MP in modern times (and also the first to bear a baby out of wedlock).*

66 It is better to die on your feet than to live on your knees. **99**

> —*Spanish firebrand* DOLORES IBARRURI, *who did neither. Pinko to the core, "La Pasionaria" survived nearly forty years of exile under Franco—and was re-elected to Parliament at the age of 81.*

66 When my public activities are reported it is very annoying to read how I looked, if I smiled, if a particular reporter liked my hairstyle. **99**

> —VIJAYA LAKSHMI PANDIT, *circa 1955. Quite perversely, the former President of the United Nations focused on what was in her head, not on it.*

66 'We, the people.' It is a very eloquent beginning. But when that document was completed on the seventeenth of September in 1787 I was not included in that 'We, the people.' I felt somehow for many years that George Washington and Alexander Hamilton just left me out by mistake. 99

66 The stakes . . . are too high for government to be a spectator sport. 99

—*Black civil rights champion* BARBARA JORDAN, *who found Congress a more comfortable place to sit than on the sidelines.*

66 I don't drink or do any drugs. I don't need them. I'm a Black woman from the land of the free, home of the brave and I figure I don't need another illusion. **99**

—BERTICE BERRY, *one ticked-off talk show host.*

66 I couldn't vote for my father, I thought he was wrong on everything. **99**

—PATTI DAVIS, *Democrat. Patti's dad, Ronnie, was a prominent Republican.*

66 If you're average and *white,* honey, you can go far. Just look at Dan Quayle. If that boy was colored he'd be washing dishes somewhere. **99**

—ANNIE ELIZABETH DELANY, DDS. *Born to a freed slave in 1891, Dr. Delany had logged 101 years in the proverbial melting pot at the time of her tart remark.*

❝ I would like to be the first ambassador to the United States *from* the United States. **❞**

> —BARBARA MIKULSKI *(D-Maryland), in 1973. Some thirteen years later, the would-be diplomat finally got her wish, metaphorically speaking, as the first woman Democrat elected to the US Senate.*

❝ I would rather have a President who does it to a woman than a President who does it to his country. **❞**

> —*The very liberal* SHIRLEY MACLAINE, *who didn't hold a grudge against JFK for attempting an unsolicited grope.*

66 Men and women are like right and left hands: it doesn't make sense not to use both. 99

—JEANNETTE RANKIN. *The first woman to serve in Congress, JR had a more ambidextrous attitude than many of her colleagues.*

66 I've had quite a lot of what might be called global experience. 99

—*The much-loved* PAMELA HARRIMAN, *appointed US Ambassador to the Land of L'Amour at the age of 73.*

❝ I'll show them how to run an orderly house. **❞**

> —*1974 campaign slogan of busy* BEVERLY HARRELL. *When not pursuing a seat in the state legislature, Madam Beverly presided over Nevada's raunchy "Cottontail Ranch."*

❝ Women are beginning to feel that they are not fairly represented. As we say, two percent may be fine for fat in milk, but not for the United States Senate. **❞**

> —*Senator* DIANNE FEINSTEIN *(D-Cal), casting a critical eye on her figure(s) in 1992—the so-called "Year of the Woman."*

66 There is not a man shortage. There is actually a man excess. Look at the House of Representatives. Look at the Senate. Look at the tenured faculty in any American college. You will see an appalling man excess, which means a woman shortage. **99**

—Time-*ly essayist* BARBARA EHRENREICH, *an expert on today's testosterone epidemic.*

66 A nonentity can be just as famous as anybody else if enough people know about him. 99

66 [Put] Congress on a commission basis. Pay them for results. If they do a good job and the country prospers, they get 10% of the extra take. 99

66 If a woman isn't qualified to be President, why is it you never see anything but pants on scarecrows? 99

—GRACIE ALLEN. *The comic candidate of the spoofy "Surprise Party," goofy Gracie got hundreds of write-in votes in 1940—though not enough, of course, to oust FDR from the Oval Office.*

66 I think it's about time we voted for senators with breasts. After all, we've been voting for boobs long enough. 99

—*Would-be congresswoman* CLAIRE SARGENT, *giving her opponent tit for tat in Arizona's 1992 campaign.*

66 Somewhere out there . . . may even be someone who will one day follow in my footsteps and preside over the White House as the president's spouse. And I wish him well. 99

—BARBARA BUSH, *who shacked up with the head of state from 1989 to 1993.*

66 We need new blood in the White House—
every twenty-eight days. 99

—*The ever-raunchy* ROSEANNE. *Time for a woman president, period.*

11.

Singular Soliloquies

66 In olden times sacrifices were made at the altar—a practice which is still continued. **99**

> —HELEN ROWLAND, *who penned* Reflections of a Bachelor Girl *in unrepentant solitude.*

66 No honey for me, if it comes with a bee. **99**

> —SAPPHO, *the odd ancient Greek who was genuinely fond of girls.*

66 I'd like to have a husband, but making babies I think is a huge penitence: your breasts hang way down and it's too anguishing to be a wife. **99**

> —*French nun* ALAIS, *who clearly appreciated the perks (not to mention the perkiness) of her celibate 12th-century lifestyle.*

66 Love is so much better when you're not married. **99**

> —*Soprano* MARIA CALLAS, *a Medea with major-scale man trouble.*

66 I want to be alone. **99**

66 I never said, 'I want to be alone.' I only said, 'I want to be *left* alone.' There is all the difference. **99**

> —GRETA GARBO. *Details, details! For better or worse, solitude certainly allowed the bisexual Swede (who dumped her dude on their wedding day) to maintain a major mystique.*

66 A positive engagement to marry a certain person at a certain time, at all haps and hazards, I have always considered the most ridiculous thing on earth. 99

—JANE CARLYLE. *Married in 1826 to a very moody man, caustic Mrs. C wasn't crazy about the post-engagement period, either.*

66 Liberty is a better husband than love to many of us. **99**

66 Girls write to ask who the little women marry, as if that was the only end and aim of a woman's life. **99**

66 It does me good to be alone. **99**

> —LOUISA MAY ALCOTT. *To please her public, the 19th-century novelist paired her fictional Little Women (even the patently butch one) off with fellows—but refused to bite the bullet in real life.*

66 This marrying I do not like: 'tis like going on a long voyage to sea, where after a while even the calms are distasteful, and the storms dangerous: one seldom sees a new object, 'tis still a deal of sea, sea; husband, husband, every day,—till one's quite cloyed with it. **99**

—APHRA BEHN. *Like many a starving scrivener in the 17th century, England's first female professional writer spent her share of time in debtor's prison. On the bright side, the spouse-averse author must have collected some magnificent matériel in the brig.*

66 Sleep around all you want, but don't get married. **99**

>—DEBRA KOENIG, *attorney-at-law, who imparted this crucial nugget of career advice to a group of seventh-grade girls on "Take Our Daughters to Work" day in 1993.*

66 If you want to sacrifice the admiration of many men for the criticism of one, go ahead, get married. **99**

>—KATHARINE HOUGHTON HEPBURN. *And indeed, Mama Hebburn's movie star daughter never wed her main man (Mrs. Spencer Tracy beat her to the punch).*

66 I would rather be a beggar and single than a queen and married. **99**

—*The vehemently virginal* QUEEN ELIZABETH I *of England. (And if Henry VIII was your dad, you'd think twice before tying the knot too.)*

66 It's like magic. When you live by yourself, all your annoying habits are gone! **99**

—*Funny girl* MERRILL MARKOE, *much improved since her stint as David Letterman's main squeeze.*

66 During your best years you don't need a husband. You do need a man of course every step of the way, and they are often cheaper emotionally and a lot more fun by the dozen. 99

66 I think a single woman's biggest problem is coping with the people who are trying to marry her off! 99

66 You can have babies until you're forty or older. And if you happen to die before *they* are forty, at least you haven't lingered into their middle age to be a doddering old bore. 99

—Cosmopolitan HELEN GURLEY BROWN, *notorious for her sexy take on the transition from Miss to Mrs. . . . er, Ms.*

" Let no one ever say that marriages are made in Heaven; the gods would not commit so great an injustice! **"**

> —QUEEN MARGUERITE *of Valois, wife of Henry IV of France. Alas, the much-loved monarch turned out to be a bust as Maggie's bridegroom, and the union was annulled in 1599.*

66 Few gynecologists recommend to their heterosexual patients the most foolproof of solutions, namely Misterectomy. **99**

> —MARY DALY, *one theologian who is unlikely to repeat herself.*

66 My husbands have been very unlucky. **99**

> —LUCREZIA BORGIA, *mistress of understatement. Guys who loved Lucy tended to disappear when her pop, Pope Alexander VI, deemed that a liaison had outlived its political purpose.*

" If I am not noble enough to be your wife, I am too much so to be your mistress. **"**

> —ANTOINETTE DE PONS GUERCHEVILLE, *who pitched a righteous fit when horny Henry IV put the moves on her. (Apparently "Queen for A Day" wasn't quite what Madame had in mind.)*

12.

Irascible
Individualists

66 I got what I have now through knowing the right time to tell terrible people when to go to hell. **99**

—LESLIE CARON. *Of course, the lissome leading lady of "An American in Paris" excelled as a hoofer as well as a harpy.*

66 Mother Teresa tries to do good, and when she sees an injustice in the world she doesn't get angry—she gets busy. Well, I'm not Mother Teresa. **99**

—LESLIE ABRAMSON, *notoriously cranky criminal attorney.*

66 The more you learn about the dignity of the gorilla, the more you want to avoid people. 99

—DIAN FOSSEY. *A serious simian wanna-be, the passionate primatologist was accepted as a peer . . . by the apes she so adored.*

66 I never know how much of what I say is true. 99

—BETTE MIDLER, *cinema's campiest coquette.*

66 Selfishness must always be forgiven, you know, because there is no hope of a cure. 99

66 I am sure of *this,* that if everybody was to drink their bottle a day, there would be not half the disorders in the world there are now. It would be a famous good thing for us all. 99

66 For what do we live, but to make sport for our neighbors, and laugh at them in our turn? 99

> —*The delightfully jaundiced* JANE AUSTEN, *posthumously the most popular author of 19th-century England.*

❝ I'll not listen to reason. Reason always means what someone else has got to say. **❞**

> —*England's* ELIZABETH GASKELL, *in her 1851 novel* Cranford—*a separatist tour de force featuring (or flaunting) a bevy of self-sufficient spinsters.*

❝ I've never thought I spoke for America. I speak for myself. That's why it says 'Liz Smith' on top of [my] space, not 'Most of America.' **❞**

> —LIZ SMITH—*a syndicated columnist, not a sycophantic one.*

66 Conventionality is not morality. Self-righteousness is not religion. To attack the first is not to assail the last. **99**

66 It is vain to say human beings ought to be satisfied with tranquillity: they must have action; and they will make it if they cannot find it. **99**

66 Better to be without logic than without feeling. **99**

> —CHARLOTTE BRONTË, *the Gothic genius who gave us* Jane Eyre. *Peculiar as it seems today, some Victorian critics considered the classic love story vulgar and even "coarse." (Probably they didn't care for "Romeo and Juliet," either.)*

66 I stopped believing in Santa Claus at an early age. Mother took me to see Santa Claus in a Hollywood department store and he asked for my autograph. 99

—SHIRLEY TEMPLE BLACK. *One assumes, of course, that the future US diplomat refrained from telling clueless Claus just what he could do with his North Pole.*

66 The schools I went to as a kid made me wary. It was clear to me that everything was a lie except math. 99

—SUSAN SHOWN HARJO—*an American Native, not a naïf.*

66 The secret of eternal youth is arrested development. **99**

66 If I err, it will not be on the side of the angels. **99**

66 They expect me to wear a halo and I only wear a hat. **99**

—ALICE ROOSEVELT LONGWORTH. *Affectionately dubbed "Washington's Other Monument," Teddy Roosevelt's rambunctious daughter raised hell in her hometown . . . for nearly nine decades.*

66 I'm a ragged individualist. **99**

—Radio personality JANE ACE, *a more realistic role model for most of us struggling wage slaves than the Marlboro Man.*

66 I think I'm fierce. But every individual on the face of this earth has the capacity for ferocity if they want it. I'm fierce, but you could be, too. **99**

—Ambitious artiste FREDI WALKER, *self-lionized as "the next Spike Lee."*

66 The thing to do is to grab the broom of anger and drive off the beast of fear. 99

66 I want a busy life, a just mind and a timely death. 99

—ZORA NEALE HURSTON, *Harlem Renaissance woman.*

66 I make enemies deliberately. They are the *sauce piquante* to my dish of life. 99

66 Brains are always awkward at a gay and festive party. 99

66 Down with boredom! 99

—Bon vivant ELSA MAXWELL, *the high society hostess of the early 20th century. Almost anything (including, on one occasion, a herd of milk cows) went at Miss Maxwell's wacky bashes—but bores were strictly verboten.*

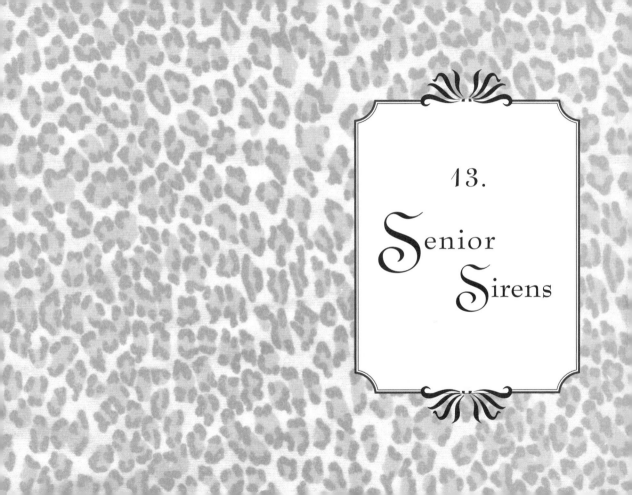

13.

Senior Sirens

66 I am at present in such health and such spirits, that when I recollect I am an old woman, I am astonished. **99**

—CATHERINE CLIVE. *Born in 1711, the London stage star curtailed her career nearly sixty years later . . . and went on to launch a highly successful salon.*

66 I am not half as patient with old women now that I am one. **99**

—*Canada's* EMILY CARR, *an increasingly nasty nature painter.*

66 I have always adored beautiful young men. Just because I grow older my taste doesn't change. So if I can still have them, why not? **99**

—*Sixties sex kitten* BRIGITTE BARDOT, *still on the prowl.*

66 I feel that you reach a certain age and then things start to jell. After I hit forty, you couldn't mess around with me so much anymore. **99**

—JULIE KAVNER, *rock-solid TV talent.*

66 My younger lusty, impecunious, and opportunistic companion and I (an aging, sagging, graying, experienced older woman), are doing our best . . . but we can't change the world single-handedly. How about declaring this 'Men, Take a Same Age or Older Woman To Lunch (Or Bed)' Week! **99**

—*San Francisco sex therapist* ISADORA ALMAN, *grandma's potential patron saint.*

66 When I'm old, I'm never going to say, 'I didn't do this,' or 'I regret that.' I'm going to say, 'I don't regret a damn thing. I came, I went, and I did it all.' 99

    —*Blond bombshell* KIM BASINGER. *Evidently a rather sentimental sort, kinky Kim once purchased an entire Georgia town abutting "the fields where I learned oral sex."*

66 When you're old, everything you do is sort of a miracle. 99

    —*Marvelous* MILLICENT FENWICK *(R–New Jersey), a civil servant into her seventies.*

66 I wasn't young, I wasn't pretty, it was necessary to find other weapons. **99**

> —*Journalist* DOMINIQUE AURY *(aka Pauline Réage). In 1954, the then-40ish Frenchwoman penned the sizzling, ultra-explicit* Story of O *solely to get her guy interested again. (And the result? Ooo la la!)*

66 If you rest, you rust. **99**

> —HELEN HAYES, *an untarnished talent during her seven decades on stage.*

66 I was born in 1962. True. And the room next to me was 1963. 99

—*Good humor woman* JOAN RIVERS, *noted for her deadpan delivery.*

66 I refuse to admit that I'm more than fifty-two even if that does make my sons illegitimate. 99

—LADY NANCY ASTOR, *an astonishingly youthful MP.*

66 It's not easy to get the weight off. I've been walking, jogging three miles a day. But you know what the best way is? Young men. 99

>   —*Flab-fighter* ARETHA FRANKLIN, *still full of soul (among other things) at fifty-something.*

66 I tell my conservative women friends who bother me about my youthful lover to 'fuck off' or go get them one of their own. 99

>   —*Actress* URSULA ANDRESS, *a great (if not entirely grammatical) inspiration to lascivious ladies on and off the screen.*

66 Honey, sex doesn't stop until you're in the grave. **99**

—*Octagenarian* LENA HORNE—*over the hill, not over the hump.*

66 I'm tired of playing worn-out depressing ladies in frayed bathrobes. I'm going to get a new hairdo and look terrific and go back to school and even if nobody notices, I'm going to be the most self-fulfilled lady on the block. **99**

—JOANNE WOODWARD. *Past her prime only in Hollywood, the aging ingenue earned a Sarah Lawrence degree in lieu of another Academy Award.*

66 Mandatory retirement ought to be illegal. **99**

66 Learning and sex until rigor mortis. **99**

—*Geriatric rabble-rouser* MAGGIE KUHN, *the Grayest Panther of them all.*

66 When you are as old as I . . . you will know there is only one thing in the world worth living for, and that is sin. **99**

> —LADY SPERANZA WILDE, *who must have passed her proclivity for perversity along to offspring Oscar.*

66 The older one grows, the more one likes indecency. **99**

> —VIRGINIA WOOLF. *And all this time we simply assumed that the bisexual Bloomsbury novelist was writing in that ever-so-symbolic room . . .*

66 I look back on my life like a good day's work; it was done and I am satisfied with it. **99**

> —Celebrity procrastinator Anna "GRANDMA" MOSES, who launched a sizzling painting career in her sixty-seventh year of life.

14.

Heretical
Hullabaloo

❝ If I was the Virgin Mary, I would have said no. **❞**

> —STEVIE SMITH. *Needless to say, the off-beat Brit who won the Queen's Gold Medal for Poetry in 1969 was blessed with a very fertile . . . imagination.*

❝ You were born God's original. Try not to become someone's copy. **❞**

> —*The inimitable* MARIAN WRIGHT EDELMAN, *dedicated director of the Children's Defense Fund.*

66 Maybe [women] weren't at the Last Supper, but we're certainly going to be at the next one. **99**

—*New York Congresswoman* BELLA ABZUG. *A mover and shaker in the women's movement of the 1960s and '70s, outspoken Abzug was known as "Battling Bella" . . . and much, much worse.*

66 There is a communion of more than our bodies when bread is broken and wine is drunk. And that is my answer when people ask me: Why do you write about hunger, and not wars or love? **99**

—*Author* MFK FISHER *on the subject of soul food.*

66 People see God every day; they just don't recognize him. **99**

—*Show biz sensation* PEARL BAILEY, *also in the public eye for most of her seven decades on earth.*

66 I became a nun, because although I recognized it as having many ramifications . . . foreign to my temperament, still, given my completely negative feelings about marriage, it was the least disproportionate and most fitting thing I could do. **99**

> —JUANA INÉS DE LA CRUZ, *circa 1691. Obviously, candid de la Cruz was not the first female to take the veil out of pure pragmatism . . . though she may have been the first to admit it.*

66 I shall never send for a priest or recite an Act of Contrition in my last moments. If the kind of God exists Who would damn me for not working out a deal with Him, then that is unfortunate. I should not care to spend eternity in the company of such a person. **99**

—*Author* MARY MCCARTHY. *A life-long lefti , daring Mary didn't cotton to the concept of dictatorship . . . even in the afterlife.*

66 I would rather believe that God did not exist than believe that He was indifferent. **99**

> —France's scandalous GEORGE SAND, *apparently accustomed to getting a lot of attention from guys.*

66 Believing in gods always causes confusion. **99**

> —*Chaos-buster* PEARL BUCK. *Like a literary Mia Farrow, the well-organized writer mothered a huge brood of adoptive children, published prodigiously to support them, and also managed to nab the 1938 Nobel prize for literature.*

66 The trouble with life isn't that there is no answer, it's that there are so many answers. 99

> —RUTH BENEDICT *(aka Anne Singleton). Proving her point, Benedict carved out comprehensive careers for herself in both anthropology and poetry (but not, one notes, in math).*

66 Change is the only constant. Hanging on is the only sin. 99

> —*Speed demon* DENISE MCCLUGGAGE, *one of the world's fastest women on (race car) wheels.*

❝ God is love, but get it in writing. **❞**

    —GYPSY ROSE LEE, *an exceptionally skeptical ecdysiast.*

❝ Christians can have big tits, too. **❞**

    —*God-fearing screen queen* JANE RUSSELL, *a woman doubly blessed.*

66 One thing I have no worry about is whether God exists. But it has occurred to me that God has Alzheimers and has forgotten we exist. **99**

66 Infinity, it could be time on an ego trip for all I know. **99**

66 What is reality, anyway? Nothing but a collective hunch. **99**

—JANE WAGNER, *the wonderfully warped mind behind many of Lily Tomlin's lines.*

66 What we call reality is an agreement that people have arrived at to make life more livable. **99**

—*Sculptor* LOUISE NEVELSON, *no great fan of the status quo.*

66 You don't get to choose how you're going to die. Or when. You can only decide how you're going to live. Now. **99**

—*Peace freak* JOAN BAEZ, *a big name in the be-here-now era.*

66 The best case scenario for me and the millennium is that smoking works, and I don't have to be there. I think it's astonishing how people just want to live long lives now. For what? **99**

—*Where there's smoke, there's . . . cigarette fiend* FRAN LEBOWITZ, *high society's ever-smoldering satirist.*

66 My teeth are good, and if I can get enough to eat, I don't know why I should die. There's no use in dying—you ain't good for anything after you are dead. 99

>—*Swine breeder* SILVIA DUBOIS *in 1883, chomping at the bit for a second century of life.*

66 Excuse my dust. 99

>—*Devastating wit* DOROTHY PARKER, *who suggested this punny epitaph for her own out-of-this-world self.*

66 Eternity is not something that begins after you are dead. It is going on all the time. We are in it now. **99**

    —CHARLOTTE PERKINS GILMAN. *Suffering, circa 1888, from marital malaise and a deep-seated desire not to clean the house, the much-lauded author of* Women and Economics *left her spouse to deal with the dirty dishes and lived happily ever after.*

66 I'll pinch you in the behind. **99**

    —ELISABETH KÜBLER-ROSS. *A pioneer in the post-mortem field, the maverick MD promised to send a special sign when she reached the other side.*

15.

Undomesticated Utterances

66 A house is not a home. **99**

> —*Madam* POLLY ADLER, *a different sort of domestic worker.*

66 The best thing that could happen to motherhood already has. Fewer women are going into it. **99**

> —*Jaded journalist* VICTORIA BILLINGS. *And next, we suppose, they'll be telling us that apple pie is passé too.*

66 I cannot help thinking that the vows most women are made to take are very foolhardy. I doubt whether they would willingly go to the altar to swear that they will allow themselves to be broken on the wheel every nine months. **99**

—SUZANNE CHARDON NECKER. *Though B&D was scarcely her MO,* saloniére *Suzanne personally produced one very distinguished daughter. Needless to say, little Germaine de Staël was groomed to take no guff from guys.*

66 By far the most common craving of pregnant women is not to be pregnant. **99**

> —Comic PHYLLIS DILLER, who celebrated the end of her childbearing years by submitting to the plastic surgeon's knife . . . seventeen times.

66 An ugly baby is a very nasty object, and the prettiest is frightful when undressed. **99**

> —QUEEN VICTORIA of England. Ironically, the monarch who lent her name to an era of extreme sexual decorum was also the mother of nine.

66 Death and taxes and childbirth! There's never any convenient time for any of them. **99**

> —*Spellbinder* MARGARET MITCHELL, *the Scheherezade who put the words in Scarlett's sassy mouth.*

66 I love all my children, but some of them I don't like. **99**

> —LILLIAN CARTER, *the proud (or possibly not) progenitor of US president #39.*

66 Parents can never do too much for their children to repay them for the injustice of having brought them into the world. 99

—*Super-suffragist* ELIZABETH CADY STANTON, *who must have spoiled her seven little suffragettes absolutely rotten.*

66 Parents have too little respect for their children, just as the children have too much for the parents. 99

—*Author* IVY COMPTON-BURNETT, *whose unhappy upbringing left her with a horror of family life . . . and seventeen novels' worth of material.*

66 A mother is not a person to lean on but a person to make leaning unnecessary. **99**

> —DOROTHY CANFIELD FISHER. *That leave-Ma-alone philosophy of parenting must have come in handy when Mrs. F was turning out yet another of her numerous tomes on . . . parenting.*

66 If you have never been hated by your child, you have never been a parent. **99**

> —*Hollywood's hallowed* BETTE DAVIS, *every bit as maternal as "Coat-Hanger Mom" Joan Crawford.*

66 The idea of feminine authority is so deeply embedded in the human subconscious that even after all these centuries of father-right the young child instinctively regards the mother as the supreme authority. **99**

> —ELIZABETH GOULD DAVIS. *One presumes, naturally, that the phrase "just wait until your father gets home" has never leapt from this fine feminist theorist's lips.*

66 Babies don't come with directions on the back or batteries that can be removed. Motherhood is twenty-four hours a day, seven days a week. You can't 'leave the office.' **99**

—*US Congresswoman* PATRICIA SCHROEDER, *a politician (and a parent) long before the advent of paternity leave.*

66 The family is a human institution: humans made it and humans can change it. 99

—SHER HITE. *Contrary to common opinion, the pop scholar posited in 1994, single moms don't necessarily scar their sons for life.*

66 Families are great murderers of the creative impulse, particularly husbands. 99

—*Author* BRENDA UELAND, *launching the backlash against an all-too-common domestic crime.*

66 The definition of woman's work is shitwork. **99**

> —GLORIA STEINEM. *The founding mother of Ms. urged fed-up females to get off the pot . . . or else.*

66 It takes just as much courage to stick to the housework until it is done as it does to go out and meet a bear. **99**

> —LOU HOOVER. *Though the fearless first lady didn't mind dodging bullets during the Boxer Rebellion, walking into the White House kitchen simply gave her the willies.*

66 Mothers and housewives are the only workers who do not have regular time off. They are the great vacationless class. 99

66 Woman's normal occupations run counter to creative life, or contemplative life or saintly life. 99

66 I believe that what a woman resents is not so much giving herself in pieces as giving herself purposelessly. 99

—ANNE MORROW LINDBERGH—*author, aviator, and (like most working moms) altogether overextended.*

66 I refuse to believe that trading recipes is silly. Tuna-fish casserole is at least as real as corporate stock. **99**

—*Journalist* BARBARA GRIZZUTI HARRISON, *bullish on bonds between women.*

66 In time your relatives will come to accept the idea that a career is as important to you as your family. Of course, in time the polar ice cap will melt. **99**

—*Cartoonist* BARBARA DALE. *More often than not, the woman who has it all has had it up to* here.

16.

Hardcore
Heroines

66 I wanted to knock her out. **99**

> —*Teen trophyist* DALLAS MALLOY, *the victor in the first official US bout between boxers with breasts. (Miss Malloy's penchant for pugilism came in handy, by the way, in her 1993 battle to sanction the sport for her sex in the first place.)*

66 When I want to really blast one, I just loosen my girdle and let 'er fly. **99**

> —BABE DIDRIKSON ZAHARIAS. *Even sadistic skivvies couldn't stifle the spirit of the world's greatest gal athlete.*

66 I would rather fight with my hands than my tongue. 99

—DOLLEY MADISON. *Fortunately, Mrs. M seldom found it necessary to resort to fisticuffs while serving as her country's first lady.*

66 When I put the shot, it's feminine, because I'm female. Athletic motion doesn't have a gender. 99

—*Studly* MAREN SEIDLER—*able-bodied, not Abel-bodied.*

66 I don't know why it should surprise people women are so tough. What I do is probably not as tough as [being] a single mother, raising two kids, and paying rent or a mortgage. **99**

—*Iditarod icon* LIBBY RIDDLES, *one woman who chose a dog's life of her own free will.*

66 When I saw something that needed doing, I did it. **99**

—*Prospector* NELLIE CASHMAN. *The feisty "Frontier Angel" struck gold six times over—then squandered her spoils on charitable causes.*

66 I rang for ice, but *this* is ridiculous! **99**

—*Unflappable world traveller* MADELINE TALMAGE ASTOR, *in the process of evacuating the Titanic.*

66 I wanted to be recognized as a good driver, not a girl driver. **99**

—*Race-car champ* SHAWNA ROBINSON. *Naturally, it was a drag when her sponsor suggested that she sport a pretty pink suit at the wheel.*

❝ Don't ever call me a jockette. **❞**

       —Jockey ROBYN SMITH*—slight of build, not self-esteem.*

❝ There are two kinds of stones, as everyone knows, one of which rolls. **❞**

       —Absentee aviator AMELIA EARHART. *Moss was not her medium.*

66 God intended woman to be outside as well as men, and they do not know what they are missing when they stay cooped up in the house with a novel. **99**

> —Hired gun ANNIE OAKLEY. *Strange but true: the celebrity sharpshooter was once solicited to end an epidemic of man-eating tigers in Senegal.*

66 Damn right, partner! **99**

> —Hold-up artist PEARL HART. *Convicted of stagecoach robbery in 1899, the candid criminal didn't mince words when asked if she'd do it again. Of course, Hart had to have the loot (so she explained) to pay her mother's medical bills.*

66 I have already improved considerably by my travels. First, I can swallow gruel soup, egg soup, and all manner of soups, without making faces much. Secondly, I can pretty well live without tea . . . 99

—*English essayist* ANNA LETITIA BARBAULD, *apparently starving for culture during her 1785 sojourn to France.*

66 It beats sitting around with my butt in a sling. 99

—*The eloquent* ANTOINETTE CANCELLO, *circus aerialist.*

66 Heart, courage, intelligence, and grace are the requirements. The bull doesn't ask to see your identity card. **99**

—Yolanda Carbajal, *a most unmanly matador.*

66 The reason I keep doing it is for the tremendous rush I get at the end. . . . I'm overwhelmed by the strength of my body and the power of my mind. For one moment, just one second, I feel immortal. **99**

—*Long-distance swimmer* Diana Nyad, *a seriously ripped sea goddess.*

66 I don't want to be graded on a curve. 99

> —*Tennis ace* MARY CARILLO, *who wouldn't dream of describing Andre Agassi as a* man *tennis ace.*

66 A precipice cannot hurt you. The streets of New York I consider more dangerous than the Matterhorn to a thoroughly competent and careful climber. 99

> —*Mountaineer* ANNIE PECK. *Though city life put a crimp in her crampons, the turn-of-the-century cliff-scaler was perfectly at home in the Himalayas.*

66 Getting hit really isn't that bad. The worst part is getting beat. **99**

> —BOBBIE LYNN BOWEN. *So much for bra-burning—boxing Bobbie struck a literal blow for sexual equality in the Seventies, snagging the title of Miss Junior Golden Gloves.*

66 I just wanted to get out of the house. That was why I turned to sports. It was the only way I could stay out past 5 o'clock. **99**

> —WILLYE B. WHITE, *whose strategy for avoiding parental scrutiny led to five Olympic medals.*

" What's a hero? I didn't even think about it. **"**

> —ULI DERICKSON. *Coffee, tea, or . . . terrorist hijackers? It was all in a day's work (well, actually, about seventeen of them) for the tenacious TWA flight attendant who negotiated her passengers' release in 1985.*

" I think a lot of people believe I'm going to fall flat on my face, and they're still waiting for it to happen. I hope they wait forever, and I hope they keep coming to watch me. **"**

> —CHRISTINE WREN. *Under severe sexist scrutiny, pro baseball's second woman ump never batted an eyelash.*

66 [Some women] go through all this effort of working out, cross-training—and then they get so depressed by some relationship that they can't even get out of bed. My agenda is: Nobody's going to fuck with my velocity. **99**

—*Fitness freak* CAROL WOLPER, *not about to let a little heart trouble throw her off track.*

66 Be bold. If you're going to make an error, make a doozy, and don't be afraid to hit the ball. **99**

> —BILLIE JEAN KING, *long the leading name in ladies' tennis. Needless to say, the Wimbledon winner who trounced a star of the opposite sex in 1973 made an impact in more ways than one.*

66 To be perfectly honest, what I'm really thinking about are dollar signs. **99**

> —*Churlish skating champ* TONYA HARDING, *a (lower) class act to the end.*

66 People are saying we're feminists. Good Lord! She just wants to be a wrestler. **99**

> —Nice old-fashioned KAREN HERRING. *In 1997, the semantically-challenged Texan threw a snit when school authorities banned her daughter from grappling with the guys.*

17.

$\mathcal{A}$d Hoc
$\mathcal{A}$utonomy

❝ Never say No when the world says Aye. **❞**

> —ELIZABETH BARRETT BROWNING. *Celebrated for her sensational love sonnets, the Victorian versifier didn't actually meet Mr. Right until the age of forty. (Even then, life wasn't all hearts and flowers: so disagreeable did Lizzie's dad find her famous beau that he literally never spoke to her again.)*

❝ Life shrinks or expands in proportion to one's courage. **❞**

> —ANAÏS NIN. *The* pièce de *(least)* résistance *in a star-spangled literary circle, little Nin liked to live big—and also, it turns out, bigamously.*

66 Nothing in life is to be feared. It is only to be understood. 99

—MARIE CURIE. *Canny Madame C captured one Nobel Prize for catching on to the concept of radioactivity, and another for her comprehension of chemistry.*

66 One can never consent to creep when one feels an impulse to soar. 99

—*The oft-heralded* HELEN KELLER, *a notably non-creepy humanitarian.*

66 The great thing to learn about life is, first, not to do what you don't want to do, and, second, to do what you do want to do. **99**

— MARGARET ANDERSON. *A leading literary light of the early 1900s, artsy Anderson renounced the bourgeois "joys of country clubs and bridge" and marriage for a life of literature and lesbian love.*

66 I don't eat junk foods and I don't think junk thoughts. **99**

— PEACE PILGRIM, *a rather puritanical pacifist.*

66 I do want to get rich but I never want to do what there is to do to get rich. **99**

66 Everything is so dangerous that nothing is really very frightening. **99**

66 There ain't no answer. There ain't going to be any answer. There never has been an answer. That's the answer. **99**

—*Author* GERTRUDE STEIN. *Original to a fault, Stein's exceedingly experimental prose raised plenty of questions . . . and plenty of hackles as well.*

❝ Before you can be eccentric you must know where the circle is. **❞**

　　—*Leading lady* ELLEN TERRY, *whose propensity to have babies without benefit of marriage kept her on the outskirts of English society.*

❝ Healthy people aren't that interesting. **❞**

　　—*Playwright* MARY GALLAGHER, *always up for a little psycho drama.*

66 If your head tells you one thing and your heart tells you another, before you do anything, you should first decide whether you have a better head or a better heart. **99**

> —*Sagacious* MARILYN VOS SAVANT, *the uncommon genius with great common sense.*

66 Boredom is a great motivator. **99**

> —*Self-helpful* UMA THURMAN, *whose sure cure for ennui (so she maintains) is the conquest of a hunky co-star.*

66 The mind can absorb no more than the seat can endure. 99

> —JANET TRAVELL, *the matronly MD whose peculiar prescription for physical therapy rocked JFK's socks.*

66 Nothing is so good as it seems beforehand. 99

> —*Noted novelist* GEORGE ELIOT. *Raised to be religious, Girl George also was not so good as she seemed before she started living in sin.*

66 The beauty of the past belongs to the past. **99**

> —MARGARET BOURKE-WHITE. *Pretty was entirely beside the point for the photojournalist who documented the devastation of World War II.*

66 Where there is money, there is fighting. **99**

> —*Diva* MARIAN ANDERSON, *hitting a philosophical note.*

66 Nothing that costs only a dollar is worth having. **99**

> —ELIZABETH ARDEN, *cosmetics tycoon. Demure but driven, ambitious Arden changed the face of America . . . and made herself millions in the process.*

66 It is good to get drunk once in a while. What else is there to do? **99**

> —*Poet* LI YEH, *the life of the party in 8th-century China.*

66 We don't believe in rheumatism and true love until after the first attack. 99

66 How happy are the pessimists! What joy is theirs when they have proved there is no joy. 99

66 Fear not those who argue but those who dodge. 99

—*Austria's* MARIE VON EBNER ESCHENBACH, *an aphorist with* attitude.

66 If I have learned anything, I owe it neither to precepts nor to books, but to a few opportune misfortunes. **99**

> —*Prodigious penpal* LOUISE HONORINE DE CHOISEUL, *who evidently aced her courses at the* Academie de *Hard Knocks in 18th-century France.*

66 Making the best of things is . . . a damn poor way of dealing with them. **99**

> —*Rebellious* ROSE WILDER LANE. *Her pioneer parent specialized, by contrast—so one gathers from the crisis-intensive* Little House *series by Laura Ingalls Wilder—in the search for the silver lining.*

66 It's pretty hard to retain the characteristics of one's sex after a certain age. **99**

66 Don't ever wear artistic jewellery; it wrecks a woman's reputation. **99**

66 What a wonderful life I've had! I only wish I'd realized it sooner. **99**

—*The wise and witty* COLETTE, *one of France's finest exports.*

66 What else is there to say but everything? **99**

> —GWENDOLYN BROOKS. *Far from an ivory tower type, the first black poet to win a Pulitzer Prize considered "the halls of a housing project" a fine forum for her work.*

66 Keep breathing. **99**

> —*A snippet of inspirational advice from* SOPHIE *("Last of the Red Hot Mamas")* TUCKER.

$\mathcal{I}$ndex

WILD WOMEN ASSOCIATION

In 1992, with the publication of *Wild Women* by Autumn Stephens, Conari Press founded the Wild Women Association. Today there are over 3,000 card-carrying Wild Women in cities throughout the world—and some even meet regularly with their untamed and uproarious sisters specifically to encourage unbridled behavior. The Association's primary purpose is to rediscover and rewrite our wild predecessors back into history. If there is a Wild Woman in your family, please help by sending us information for possible inclusion in subsequent volumes of the "Wild and Ever-So-Uppity Women" series!

To become a member and to receive the Wild Women Association Newsletter, please mail this page to:

The Wild Women Association
2550 Ninth Street, Suite 101
Berkeley, CA 94710-2551

Let's rewrite history with women in it!